What We Owe the Water: A Call for a Fossil Fuel Treaty

First published in 2026 by Australia Institute Press

ISBN 978-1-7636621-9-3 (print)
ISBN 978-1-7642205-0-7 (ebook)

Published in Australia and New Zealand by
Australia Institute Press
www.australiainstitute.org.au

Cataloguing-in-publication data is available from the National Library of Australia

Copyedited by Rod Morrison

Printed and bound in Australia by McPherson's Printing Group, an accredited ISO AS/NZS 14001 Environmental Management Systems printer.

What We Owe the Water: A Call for a Fossil Fuel Treaty

Kumi Naidoo

Australia Institute Press

We Come from Water

For much of my childhood, the ocean was less a place than an idea — something we knew was there, just a short drive away, yet never quite within reach.

I was born in a South Africa carved up by apartheid, where geography was not neutral, and where land and water were divided by race. In the early 1980s my family moved to Chatsworth, a working-class Durban township for Indian-origin families, about 15 kilometres from the coast. Many families were uprooted from their mixed residential suburbs and "dumped" in Chatsworth to make way for a whites-only neighbourhood. We lived close enough to smell the salt in the air on a windy day, but far enough away that the sea might as well have belonged to another world.

Even though Durban's shoreline is dotted with public beaches, apartheid decided who could set foot on which stretch of sand and who could not. The prime beaches — those with lifeguards, smooth walkways and calm, safe swimming areas — were reserved for white people. These polished and patrolled spaces were considered paradise. Hotels and restaurants lined their shores, built and serviced by Black (African, Coloured and Indian) workers who were forbidden from enjoying the beauty they helped maintain. The beaches set aside for the rest of us were fewer, harder to reach and often unsafe, with rougher currents and scant facilities. The closest that Black people could get to the "white" beaches was by driving along the narrow main road that meandered along the coast — while being carefully monitored by the police.

The ocean was not a playground for me. It was something withheld — a constant reminder of where we did not belong. Despite this, most working-class families managed a day or two at one of the "non-white" beaches during the Christmas holidays. We tried to make the best of it; sometimes hard to do as our parents were terrified of the heavy currents and backwash that saw many drownings each year.

Under the *Reservation of Separate Amenities Act*, the South African state policed everything, even the simple act of swimming. If any of us dared venture onto a white beach, we could be fined or arrested. As a child, I couldn't understand how the same ocean, endlessly moving and indivisible, could be segregated. The injustice seemed absurd: how could anyone own the waves? Rigorously enforcing the segregation of beaches to prevent people of different races swimming in the same water struck me then — as it does today — as ridiculous.

Yet even withheld, even from a distance, water was ever-present in my imagination. Its very inaccessibility gave it power. Standing on a hill or a roadside lookout, glimpsing the shimmer of the Indian Ocean, the sea represented a freedom we were denied. It stirred something in me I could not yet name — the idea that life could be larger than the fences around us, and that beyond apartheid's geography of control lay a world uncontained. The ocean was both near enough to see and impossibly far away. And in that contradiction, I learnt one of my first lessons about justice: what is denied to some is often hoarded by others.

In 1983, due to a terrible drought that devastated our province, the government imposed strict water usage limits across the greater Durban area. Households were limited to 400 litres per day, the use of hoses was banned, and those found to be in violation of the regulations faced stiff fines. This affected everyone but had a particularly devastating effect on those living in council flats and duplexes in Chatsworth and other poor areas. Many of these dwellings had communal water meters servicing up to eight homes. The monthly water bill was based on the consumption of the entire block then divided equally by the number of dwellings, with each household paying an equal share. Those living alone, mostly older people with low pension incomes, used relatively little water, but found themselves paying the same amount as extended family households, of which there were many. It was common for grandparents and other relatives to all live under one roof.

The drought and the fines put unbearable strain on the finances of the poorest households and caused considerable distress and unrest within the community. Water restrictions led to health problems and hardship, especially for the sick, the elderly and the most overcrowded households.

When I think back to those days, I remember not only the thirst and the anger, but also an awakening of my social consciousness. I was still a teenager when, along with my neighbours, we mobilised against the unfair fines that were punishing those who could least afford it. One humid afternoon, two bus-loads of people from our community — mostly women, pensioners and young people — stood outside the local council office, holding hand-painted signs demanding fair access to water. We weren't seasoned activists; we were simply tired of being punished for our imposed poverty. That protest taught me that justice isn't only about grand ideals — it's about who gets to drink, who gets to bathe, and who gets to live with dignity.

This was one of my first lessons in what we now call climate justice. Long before I understood what that term meant, I knew instinctively that the struggle for water was a struggle for life itself. The drought in our province and the rising seas in the Pacific Ocean are two verses of the same song — a song about inequality, about who bears the cost of others' excess, and about the power of ordinary people to say "enough".

It was manifestly unfair that people were being deprived of water and fined in my province. If people did not pay their fines, their water was cut off or their taps were fitted with "tricklers" which restricted the flow. If you were on the top floor of a three-storey apartment block it could take more than an hour to fill a 5-litre bucket. Those most affected by the state's punitive measures were among the poorest people in the community. We were also painfully aware that people who relied on rivers, streams and ponds for their daily water needs now had no water at all because many of those water sources had dried up.

—

My activist's journey began in earnest at the age of 15 when I witnessed first-hand the inequality of the South African education system. The government invested heavily in schooling for white kids but not for children from the broader Black community. I was expelled from school for leading protests against apartheid education. But in return, I learnt how to think critically, unlike the rote learning we were subjected to.

These experiences helped me develop and engage in other struggles my people faced. Over the ensuing decades — along with the intergenerational knowledge I gained from meeting and discussing these issues with other young and old people — I learnt about the deep connection between democracy, human rights and environmental justice.

In July 2015, five months before the Paris Agreement, I stood alongside people from Pacific Island nations to learn about what we should be doing. Listening to people from Vanuatu and Fiji and Pacific Island communities in Australia and Aoetorea/New Zealand describe the slow violence of the rising tides, I felt the weight of yet another invisible string — the profound relationship we all have with water. The water that apartheid and inequality had once denied my community was part of the same ocean now threatening to erase entire nations.

As I listened to Pacific Islanders describe their daily struggles, I heard echoes of the mothers in Durban who carried buckets up steep hills because the taps had run dry. Different geographies, same injustice. Whether in Durban or

Tuvalu, inequality always dictates who suffers first and who decides what is "affordable". These experiences taught me that water injustice is the clearest expression of moral imbalance in our world: it flows where power allows it to, not where it is needed most. Injustice had simply shifted its shape — from one region to another, from one generation to the next.

I also began to understand that the struggle for justice is always bigger than the borders we are born into. My path began in a township, not far from the beach, but it carried me across continents and oceans, into solidarity with those who live on the water's edge. Their fight to defend their homelands against the rising seas became part of my own fight — because whether denied by apartheid laws or drowned by fossil fuel emissions, the loss of water is also a loss of dignity, of memory, and of the future.

—

When I arrived in the Pacific, it was as if the ocean itself opened a new chapter of my life. Flying over scattered atolls and islands, I was struck by how vast the blue was, and how fragile the land appeared against it. For someone who had grown up cut off from the sea, the Pacific felt like a revelation — a reminder that the world is mostly water, and that to understand our planet's fate, we must understand what happens here.

In July 2015, I was asked by The Australia Institute to help them internationalise their "No New Coal Mines" campaign. I used my leave, and the Institute used its funds and capacity to get me to Kiribati to present the idea for a moratorium to then-president Anote Tong. That meeting led to the first request for a moratorium on new coal mines from the head of a nation state. President Tong's request was a move up the diplomatic ladder. Presidents and high-ranking officials can ignore a letter from anyone, even billionaires and rock stars, but the head of a nation state writing to you demands a response.

On my trip, I met communities in Kiribati, Vanuatu and Fiji who had done almost nothing to cause our contemporary climate crisis yet were being forced to fight its most immediate battles. Families told me how saltwater crept into their taro patches, how they used sandbags to hold back the tides, how the graves of their ancestors were being washed away. These were not abstract statistics. They were stories spoken of with dignity and grief, grounded by the direct lived experience of rising seas. But I also witnessed astonishing resilience: two women who lived close to the water's edge in Kiribati joked about how their pots were washed into the sea during one of the "king tides" and how they were taking bets whether those pots would ever make it back to them.

What moved me most was that these Pacific Islanders did not respond to the crisis with despair. Instead, leaders and communities chose courage. They spoke not only of survival, but of justice. Together, they demanded that the world's biggest polluters take responsibility, and that we chart a new course away from fossil fuels. Their call was clear: we cannot accept a future where entire nations are lost to the ocean.

Standing with Pacific Islanders is an act of solidarity. It stems from the recognition that the same systems of exploitation that had stolen water and land from my people in South Africa were now threatening the very existence of these island nations. Over and over again, their battle cry echoed: to save the Pacific is to save the world. The rising seas that endanger them are the same seas that connect us. Their frontline is our frontline. And in their courage, I heard the echo of my own struggles back home: a reminder that justice, like water, ignores territorial borders.

In the Pacific, water is much more than a backdrop. It is a relative, a bridge, a protector, and sometimes a destroyer. To live on its islands is to live in intimate relationship with the ocean — to know its moods, its rhythms, its deep blue silences, and its sudden fury. I learnt that the ancestors of Pacific Islanders voyaged across the ocean's vastness in canoes, guided only by starlight and memory. They trusted the waters to carry them, and in return they showed it reverence. From generation to generation, these people passed down chants, gifts and rituals that kept alive the understanding that the water is alive too.

I often think about this relationship when I am standing on a shoreline. The same ocean that has fed and held the people of the Pacific for millennia is changing before their eyes. The tides are higher, the storms more violent, the saltwater creeps further inland destroying their crops and claiming their homes. For some, the ocean has evolved from a cradle into a threat.

But that is a limited point of view. Water is not the threat. Water is the messenger. It heralds a truth about the fossil fuel age: that the burning of coal, oil and gas has consequences far beyond the cities where it happens, that the heat trapped in the atmosphere does not respect borders, and that the Pacific — vast, powerful and seemingly eternal — is now holding up a mirror to the horrors of humanity's actions.

Long before the world spoke of "climate change" or "carbon budgets", Pacific Islanders understood the fragile balance between life and the elements. They lived within cycles, not outside them. Water was not a commodity, but a relative — a living and breathing being, filled with energy, stories and inherent rights.

In Hawai'i, the ocean is known as *kai*, and freshwater is *wai* — so precious that the word for abundance is *waiwai*, a doubling of water's name. Across Polynesia, Micronesia and parts of Melanesia, the word *moana* means "ocean" or "sea". *Moana* brings people together and describes a shared world of voyaging, kinship and care. In Fiji, the common word is *wasawasa*, yet *moana* is embraced too, especially in the regions whose people speak of the "Blue Pacific". In the Marshall Islands, people say *aelōñ kein* — "our atolls" — not as possessions, but as kin to whom they belong.

Right across the region, separation between the ecological and the spiritual blurs. Water connects land to sky, ancestors to descendants, and past to future. The Pacific is not an empty space between islands. It is a living web. It is home.

This worldview shaped entire systems of governance, navigation and law. Traditional fishing zones were managed collectively while complex rites regulated when and where one could harvest the bounty of the seas. The tides and lunar phases were their calendars. The wind served as their counsel. The sea became their teacher.

This is the inheritance of the Pacific. Memories not written on paper, but carried in chants, dances, carvings and even in the stars. These are memories of balance and of equity. And they stand in stark contrast to the world that came after: a world built on extraction, on lines drawn across maps, on wealth measured not in water, but in oil.

The story of climate breakdown, then, is not just about emissions. It is about the disruption of relationships — the breaking of the covenant between humans and the natural world. And nowhere is that rupture more visible than in the rising seas now swallowing the lands that hold these ancient stories.

For the Pacific, the climate crisis is not an abstract, theoretical threat. It is a lived reality, unfolding in real time. But it is also a call — to remember, to resist and to reimagine what it means to live well with water. And to hope.

Wounds in the Water

In Western and mainstream media, an island in the Pacific usually draws on the following imagery: lush palm trees, alluring beaches and greenery, and exotic customs. The dominant narrative paints a clear image of the Pacific being paradise.

Through this type of generic symbolism, the global community has grown accustomed to certain depictions of the Pacific.[1] While on the one hand, such imagery evokes a sense of belonging and identity that Pacific Islanders view positively, on the other, it enables the commodification of the Pacific as paradise for the consumption of foreigners. It also facilitates neocolonisation.

I am talking about imagery here because I want to paint a picture. One of beauty and one of a scarring history — tainted with Western extractivist and capitalist practices. For Pacific Island nations, their home being paradise meant it was ripe for colonial exploitation.

Early European explorers fetishised the Pacific Islands as the last untouched paradise. However, today, with ever-increasing climatic catastrophes, the Pacific may start to resemble a lost or sinking paradise. This might lead one to think that agency is foreign to Indigenous Pacific Islanders and that they have no control over their circumstances. One might even regard local communities as victims who need to be saved.

Australia's relationship with Pacific Island nations has historically been complicated.[2] As a source of goods, "labour" and ideas, the Pacific Ocean served as a critical link between the young Australian colony and Britain. But a little later in history, the Pacific came to embody Australia's imperial ambitions. Such ambitions led Australia to take on a dominant role in the region, often with the assistance of a global ally. From the 19th to early 20th century, the United Kingdom was Australia's partner in this mission; from the 1940s onwards, the partner with whom it pursued its imperial aspirations has been the United States. More recently, Australia's relationship with its Pacific neighbours has revolved around the neocolonial distribution of aid, while Australia continues to exert commercial dominance. The approach can best be described as patronising.

But Australia is not alone. Since the first tests at Bikini Atoll in 1946, various Western nations including the United States, the United Kingdom and France occupied land in the Pacific in order to develop their nuclear capabilities.[3] Tests were conducted at the cost of the Indigenous people's health and the land they steward. A total of 315 nuclear detonations occurred in the Pacific between 1946 and 1958.[4] The United States alone conducted 67 tests in the Marshall Islands.

The catastrophic environmental damage ensured immediate and long-term effects on both survivors and their children. Many suffered irreparable DNA damage, as well as damage to mucosal surfaces, skin and hair, and internal organs. Pacific Islanders experienced nausea, vomiting, diarrhoea, pancytopenia and cataracts. Long-term radiation exposure has led to birth defects and genetic syndromes resulting in various cancers, such as that of the lungs, breast and thyroid; as well as leukemia and lymphoma. There were also profound psychological effects, in part caused by the loss of ancestral lands and cultural identity. While the physical health effects of radiation exposure are well-documented, the psychological trauma and the profound cultural loss are not as comprehensively recorded, but they are arguably even more serious.

—

It is a truism that planet Earth is in a perilous state. Our seas are rising, endangering the communities who depend on them, but ironically those who have contributed the least to the climate catastrophe. As climate change continues to accelerate, the urgency to act has never been more glaring. The Secretary-General of the United Nations, António Guterres, has described the situation as "code red". He has called for immediate, decisive action to avert an apocalyptic future.[5] With 2024 being the hottest year on record and the first with average global temperatures of more than 1.5°C above pre-industrial levels, humanity is edging closer to irreversible damage unless our course is radically shifted.

In recent years extreme heatwaves have gripped regions from Africa to North America, leading to devastating bushfires, destruction of property and livestock, and significant health impacts. The 2019–2020 bushfire season in Australia was one of most intense on record, while severe flooding wreaked havoc in places like the Philippines and Pakistan, displacing millions and damaging infrastructure critical for survival and recovery. These events not only destroy lives but also threaten global food security and exacerbate existing inequalities. Extreme climate events are no longer an occasional concern but a daily reality demanding our immediate attention.

As global temperatures have exceeded the 1.5°C threshold, fossil fuel expansion continues apace worldwide. The continuous operation of existing fossil fuel projects — and the commissioning of new projects — will produce emissions that exceed the carbon budget for limiting global temperature increases for years to come.

It is no exaggeration to say humanity is in a do-or-die moment.

In 2017, *The Pacific Climate Warriors Declaration on Climate Change*, a document written by climate activists representing 12 Pacific Island nations, called for urgent measures to address the crisis.[6] While acknowledging there was no "silver bullet", they suggested a range of adaptation measures that put humanity first. The declaration included calling for the phasing out of fossil fuels, financial support for climate-related loss and damage, and stricter adherence to the 2015 Paris Agreement targets. Fundamentally, it advocated for people over profits and polluters.

The declaration reflects the aspirations of Pacific Islanders as they battle the effects of the climate crisis, especially rising sea levels which will mean being forced from their land, disruption of their culture and loss of their identity. A warming and acidifying ocean and the declining health of its marine life are direct consequences of climate change. The health of the ocean not only drives the health of small island states, it affects their very future.

The health of Indigenous peoples and their land is compromised by richer, more powerful states driven by hunger for more fossil fuel extraction. The Intergovernmental Panel on Climate Change (IPCC) has found that small, low-lying island states are among the most susceptible.[7] Due to their natural exposure and their limited ability to adapt, islands with minimal elevation, especially atolls, are at particular risk of storms and flooding.

Beyond their physical and geographical characteristics, small island states' socioeconomic conditions also make them vulnerable. This in turn can lead to worsening socioeconomic inequality. The climate crisis is affecting where people can live, how often they can plant and harvest crops, and how they catch fish.

In 2024, leaders of 56 nations gathered in Apia, Samoa, for the Commonwealth Heads of Government Meeting (CHOGM). The report *Uncommonwealth: Fossil Fuel Expansion in the Commonwealth Dominated by Three Wealthy Countries* revealed the imbalance in fossil fuel extraction, with emphasis on the dominance of three rich nations — Australia, Canada and the United Kingdom — in driving fossil fuel expansion and emissions.[8]

Commonwealth countries have collectively emitted nearly 170 billion tonnes of emissions since the Rio Summit in 1992, when the climate crisis was first officially acknowledged. However, countries in the lower and lower middle-income brackets have been responsible for extracting less than 30% (48 billion tonnes), while the "Big

Three" have emitted 91 billion tonnes — over half the Commonwealth total.

Yet despite historic responsibility, and vociferous claims of concern about both Pacific Island nations and the health of the planet, the Big Three look set to dominate both fossil fuel extraction and emissions well into the future. Australia, the Pacific Islands' closest neighbour, continues to persistently expand its coal and gas sector.

Globally, Australia's fossil fuel exports are second only to Russia in terms of emissions.[9] While Australia is a large consumer of fossil fuels, it is an even larger exporter, ensuring continued reliance on fossil fuels across the Asia-Pacific region and beyond. Despite the country's high use of coal for domestic electricity generation, the fossil fuels that Australia sells overseas are responsible for a far greater amount of climate pollution each year than is emitted from the country itself. Australia has the highest emissions intensity of any developed country in the world.

In 1990, when the IPCC released its *First Assessment Report* outlining the risk of climate change, the burden of Australia's exported fossil fuels was half that of the country's domestic emissions. At the time, almost all of Australia's fossil fuel exports were coal, with just a small amount of oil and gas. This export burden doubled between 1990 and 2005, with domestic emissions and the exported emissions burden becoming roughly equal in 2005.

This growth was driven almost exclusively by increases in coal exports, though there was a significant — and temporary — increase in the country's exports of oil and oil products. Between 2005 and 2020, Australia's exported climate harm doubled again, driven by a massive increase in both coal and gas exports.

As of late 2023, 69 new coal projects and 49 new oil and gas projects were under consideration by the Australian government. Should they proceed, they would result in nearly 5 GtCO2eq (global net anthropogenic greenhouse gas emissions or GHG) by 2030. In comparison, the entire European Union's emissions for 2024 were 3 GtCO2eq. Australia's population is 6% of that of the European Union.

Australia's 2030 target is to reduce emissions by 43% below 2005 levels. Yet the Australian government continues to stress that its fossil fuel resources — particularly coal and gas — are needed for domestic and regional energy security. In 2023, the Minister for Resources emphasised that coal and gas would be "needed for decades".[10] And in 2025, the Minister attributed security and peace in the Indo-Pacific to Australia's fossil fuel exports.[11]

The accelerating scale of the climate crisis has not tempered the Australian government's appetite for approving fossil fuel projects. The situation is not helped by a suite of weak environmental laws. Since 2021 Australia has permitted 30 new coal and gas projects to proceed under the federal *Environment Protection and Biodiversity Conservation Act 1999*, which is the country's primary environmental law. From September 2024 to March 2025, the Australian government approved seven coal mine extensions that will produce a combined 828 million tonnes of coal. These extensions will lead to a further 2.1 billion tonnes of emissions over their combined operating lives.

In November 2025, Australia surrendered its bid to co-host the 31st Conference of Parties to the United Nations Framework Convention on Climate Change (COP31) along with its Pacific

Island neighbours. COPs meet annually to shape global climate policy. Pacific Island nations have been at the forefront of global climate negotiations at previous COPs and were instrumental in securing commitments such as the 1.5°C target at the 2015 Paris Agreement. Pacific Island nations' persistent advocacy underscores the existential threat they face. Pacific leaders have been deeply disappointed by Australia's decision to back away from co-hosting COP31.

Yet how is it that the Australian government frequently talks about "standing with the Pacific" while simultaneously continuing to approve new fossil fuel projects? If Australia truly wants to "stand with the Pacific", it must follow the leadership of the Pacific and commit to phasing out fossil fuels.

Nature does not negotiate. Scientists have been warning us of the threat of climate change for decades, but those in power — both in government and big business — refuse to put a brake on the industries that are driving global warming. I used to think the system was broken, but now I believe the system is working exactly as it was designed to: to benefit a small minority at the expense of the majority.

Greed, what some people have termed "affluenza", is driving humanity to the point of extinction. We continue to ignore its harms at our peril. The brutality of our economic system that ignores the pain of the poor cannot continue to go unchecked; we need action on a scale and at a pace we have never seen before.

In March 2023, Vanuatu was hit by two catastrophic cyclones within two days. In early 2025, Australia experienced an unusual and severe cyclone season. The climate crisis does not recognise borders and Australia's fossil fuel expansion directly affects its neighbours.

The climate crisis is an urgent global issue, one tied deeply with the ocean. In the islands of the Pacific, the oppression, exploitation and marginalisation stemming from colonialism has exacerbated existing vulnerabilities. Colonial power imbalances that persist today mean developing Pacific Island states must bear the brunt of climate change for which they are not responsible. Meanwhile, more powerful countries face few consequences.

But while Pacific Island peoples call for mitigation and adaptation, and foreign actors are promoting migration and relocation, there is growing resistance. The people of Pacific Island states reject the narrative of them "drowning". Even if dominant Western countries pay no mind whether the Pacific Islands continue to exist or not, a growing movement of concerned citizens will not allow this to happen. The way forward requires community action, Indigenous leadership, international cooperation and support.

Tuvalu and Vanuatu have spearheaded the call for an ambitious legal mechanism that can help protect their land; while Fiji, Vanuatu and Samoa have pushed for legal action against major polluters through a new international crime of "ecocide".

Australia has channelled millions of dollars of grants to Pacific Island nations for climate adaptation, disaster preparedness, nature-based solutions and projects which respond to loss and damage. This finance is crucial for Pacific Island nations to implement the policies and infrastructure needed to combat the effects of rising sea levels and extreme weather events. However, focusing on addressing the effects and not working to prevent their cause suggests Australia is comfortable allowing Pacific Island nations to serve as the unfortunate collateral damage of its continued dependence on fossil fuels.

A true partnership between Australia and Pacific Island states would see Australia committing to no new fossil fuel project approvals and scaling down existing production in line with the 1.5°C target, while simultaneously supporting its Pacific neighbours with the just transition they are working towards.

For more than a decade, Pacific Island nations have shown the world what true leadership looks like. While major emitters debate timelines, countries like Vanuatu, Tuvalu, Fiji and Samoa have spoken with moral clarity: no more fossil fuels and a fair plan to phase them out. Their courage is humbling. It is a reminder that those with the least material wealth often carry the greatest moral wealth. Australia has a choice — to stand as a neighbour in solidarity, or to stand aside as a bystander to history.

When the Rivers Rise

The concept of a fighting chance to save a drowning home is not new to me.

In April 2022, heavy rainfall and flooding in Durban in South Africa resulted in one of the worst natural disasters in the country's history. My province was devastated. The Hindu temple where my parents took my siblings and me as children was washed away. Videos showed pieces of the walls and the dome of the temple bobbing in the swollen river, carried off by the current. It was a grim reminder of the fragility and impermanence of what we carry closest and deepest in our hearts, and how easily everything and everyone can be destroyed.

With 544 casualties, 42,000 people displaced and 140,000 people affected, the 2022 floods raised questions about the role that climate change played in the devastation. Scientists found the extreme rainfall was linked to global warming and that it was 40% to 107% heavier than it would have been before the shift in climate.[12]

Public resources in South Africa are always stretched and the effects of extreme weather events hit the most vulnerable communities the hardest. The economic losses from the floods were staggering. Major production facilities, logistics routes and informal settlements were left submerged. Floodwaters destroyed machinery, interrupting production.

I went to Durban a month after the floods to work on a documentary called *Temperature Rising*. In Tongaat, I met local leaders who had no water — and wouldn't for the next eight months thanks to a combination of flood damage and poor maintenance. These people were completely on their own and with little government support they had to rely on their own resilience and determination. The community-led Palmiet River Watch had urged residents to immediately evacuate their homes and ignore the inaccurate forecasts on the news and by officials. Locals also relied on the Severe Weather and Information Centre SAs (a public group dedicated to accurate, real-time weather updates) for their high-level warnings. These community initiatives saved many from total catastrophe.

The power of grassroots solidarity struck me again in early 2025 when the east coast of Australia was devastated by Cyclone Alfred. I was in the Northern Rivers region of New South Wales at the time and met with Lismore resident Aidan Ricketts. Aidan told me the devastating 2022 floodwaters that inundated the region were some 2.5 metres higher than the previous all-time record. The floods were so bad they completely incapacitated the official emergency services.

With little outside help available, the community got to work. In his small boat, Aidan went out and rescued neighbours who were clinging to their roofs. He wasn't the only one. Hundreds of boats, kayaks and jet skis hit the water spontaneously to help people who were stranded. While some community members piloted the vessels, others offered a towel or blanket, took people into their homes, or gave them food. Aidan said that it was well beyond anything the government would have done.

As heartwarming as the stories of neighbours helping each other out are, extreme weather events that displace entire regions and cause tragic loss of life must not be just chalked up to a lesson on "community resilience". These events are grim reminders of how Australia's fossil fuel dependence is harming its very own people.

The New South Wales town of Lismore was still recovering from the effects of the 2022 floods when Cyclone Alfred broke records in the region yet again. Nearly 450,000 homes and businesses across New South Wales and South-East Queensland endured days without power. Heavy rainfall overwhelmed drains, causing rivers to exceed their containment thresholds, resulting in major flooding in low-lying areas. Debris and fallen trees blocked roads, businesses lost livestock, infrastructure and beaches were damaged, homes and forests were destroyed, and dead marine life washed ashore as floodwaters depleted oxygen levels in the sea.

Just like the 2022 floods in Durban, scientists agreed that anthropogenic climate change had influenced Cyclone Alfred's unpredictable and erratic behaviour.

—

Around 2012, the New South Wales state government granted several mining companies exploration licences for the Northern Rivers region. The local community was outraged and formed the Bentley Blockade, an anti-coal and gas protest movement. This represented a turning point in coal and gas expansion in Australia. Aidan Ricketts was a key organiser of the Bentley Blockade and said what shocked many people was how they managed to mobilise such widespread community support across the region. From environmentalists, townsfolk, farmers, First Nations peoples, to professionals and businesspeople — all were united by the common vision of a gas field free region.

After two years of campaigning, the Bentley Blockade was victorious. Having kicked the fossil fuel industry out of the area, Lismore is today home to one of the largest anti-fracking movements in the country. Mitigation no longer means just coming to each other's rescue. Climate justice means no one gets left behind.

Laws of the Sea, Law of Justice

Healthy oceans and seas are of fundamental importance for those who have been stewarding them for millennia.

Water covers 71% of the Earth's surface and nearly 64% (two-thirds) of the global ocean is categorised as "high seas", meaning they are outside the jurisdiction of any one country. With all this water, 152 countries are considered "coastal states", including 39 "Small Island Developing States (SIDS)" and 18 are "Associated Members of United Nations regional commissions".[13]

Coastal states exercise their sovereign rights in maritime zones measured from their coastlines — otherwise known as their exclusive economic zones or EEZs — but rising sea levels and coastal erosion are challenging our understanding of how these zones operate. EEZs currently have a maximum width of 200 nautical miles (370 kilometres). They give states jurisdiction only over the natural resources that may be present, like fish and other marine life. EEZs differ from a state's "territorial waters", which have a maximum width of only 12 nautical miles (22 kilometres), but over which the state has full sovereignty. States are able to regulate activities within their own EEZs, but since the oceans are all interconnected, the activities of any one state naturally affects another.

Around 1,700 marine species are considered vulnerable, endangered, or critically endangered according to the International Union for the Conservation of Nature (IUCN) Red List database. This means that those who rely on marine animals for their food and broader economy are being confronted by huge difficulties. Vulnerable coastal populations have long faced increased risks to their social and economic development — but legal frameworks for international cooperation and global governance are not being implemented.

Take for example the United Nations Convention on the Law of the Sea (UNCLOS). This convention was adopted in 1982 as "the constitution of the sea" and was designed to regulate human activity in the oceans and oblige states to protect and preserve the marine environment.

In 2024, the International Tribunal for the Law of the Sea Advisory Opinion on climate change found that the definition of "pollution" under Article 1(1)(4) of UNCLOS encompasses greenhouse gas emissions (GHG) due to their deleterious effects on the marine environment, both directly and indirectly, and that states have an obligation to take all necessary measures to prevent, reduce and control pollution.[14] But this reveals a problem with UNCLOS's jurisdiction: the convention only covers the 200 nautical miles from a state's coastline, leaving around 60% of the planet's oceans *outside* UNCLOS protections.

While they are some of the least known and least protected areas on Earth, the high seas sustain our planet's ecosystem. The urgency of protecting our ocean's sustainability is especially apparent in the Global South, due not only to coastal states being threatened with a scarcity of marine resources, but also because of a lack of ocean-based conventions that sustain global economies.[15]

Fishing is a hugely important industry in the Global South, making up over 70% of jobs for communities in Asia alone. With the focus on renewable energy, there also has been an increase in research on renewable energy production, research and bioprospecting with the high seas as their nodal zones. As of 2022, the economic potential in offshore wind farms alone — especially in areas near seas — was estimated at 3.5 billion Euros.[16]

It's clear the connection between the protection of biodiversity in the high seas, human rights and the phase-out of fossil fuels are closely linked. In response to environmental and human threats to the high seas, we have the High Seas Treaty or the Agreement on Biodiversity Beyond National Jurisdiction (BBNJ Agreement), which at the time of writing was due to come into force in January 2026.[17] This agreement was created to fill gaps in previous ocean governance mechanisms on conservation and sustainable use of marine biodiversity and resources.

It looks as though these new international agreements are in line with the goals of protecting marine life, but the tools that the environmental movement relied on for many decades do not adequately address our contemporary climate crisis. The law of the sea and climate change law operate on two different frameworks. Often, a human rights lens is missing.

Under UNCLOS, the dominance of "powerful actors" (for example, rich nations and large companies) has led to "exploitative partnership agreements" or continuous unsustainable maritime use, with limited equitable and just options for navigating such complexities.[18]

Furthermore, about 97% of all industrial fishing vessels on the high seas are flagged by these powerful actors. In the same way small island states are disproportionately affected by climate change, they are also at higher risk from inequitable practices in fishing and trade.

Despite the connection between the ocean and our planet's habitability, the ocean–climate nexus is yet to be effectively codified in international law. UNCLOS and the BBNJ Agreement are designed to protect the ocean and the high seas, but they make little direct reference to climate change. While these frameworks provide some governance over bodies of water that sustain economies, the climate crisis and the intersecting issues of social inequality that exacerbate its impacts are steadily reaching into the lives and livelihoods of those who live in coastal states.

With rising seas endangering the habitability and even the existence of Pacific Island nations, there are many legal questions that the global community has not yet answered. What are the impacts to states' EEZs and how are fishing rights affected when sea levels rise? What obligations would other states have to take in displaced populations and how would the human rights and legal status of these people be addressed?

The cumbersome and drawn-out nature of climate policy, as well as the debilitated obligations contained in such a legal framework, complicate the assigning of legal responsibility for the recompense of loss and damages that island states experience at the hand of other states with greater financial resources and greater emissions.

The international community must acknowledge its moral obligation to take action and provide restitution for the people affected by the sinking of island states.[19] They need to do this not only because of the physical and socio-economic vulnerabilities of these nations, but because such imbalances jeopardise global solidarity.

Our struggle for social justice may look

different at times, but much like the need for clearer international legal frameworks when it comes to the connection between climate and the ocean, we must also understand how another state's liberty and prosperity is connected with ours. When we amplify the call of the most profoundly affected, we uplift all of our struggles.

In 2019, a few brave and visionary Pacific Island law students came together and stood up for their people. Hailing from the Vanuatu campus of the University of South Pacific, these students knew exactly what the climate crisis meant. Having witnessed first-hand the devastating effects, they understood the consequences — not just to their communities, but to the entire world. Essentially, the students were seeking to take the world's biggest challenge, the climate emergency, to the world's highest court. Determined that their voices would be heard, they brought climate justice to the doors of the International Court of Justice (ICJ). In 2025, after years of hard work, thousands of kilometres from the students' home, the ICJ delivered its landmark Advisory Opinion on the "Obligations of states in respect of climate change".[20]

The Advisory Opinion reiterates the science that fossil fuels are the primary drivers of greenhouse gas emissions and legally obliges states to protect the environment. It goes on to say that these obligations are already embedded in existing treaties and agreements on climate change, the environment, the sea, human rights, and customary international law — meaning a state's failure to comply constitutes an internationally wrongful act.

The Advisory Opinion clarifies that states must develop, adopt and implement specific, tangible and time-sensitive measures, and define what human rights, state responsibility and climate justice mean in international law.

In my home country, young people are using their legal power in the courts to challenge the continued use of fossil fuels. In 2019, the South African government proposed developing 1500 megawatts (MW) of new coal-fired electricity generation. In November 2021, environmental and climate justice organisations took the government to court in a movement that has been dubbed the #CancelCoal case. The coalition argued that the government's plans to develop new coal plants threatened not only the rights of present and future generations of South Africans to be kept from harm, but also the rights to life, dignity, equality and the best interests of children. In 2024, the High Court ruled that the government's coal plans were unlawful, invalid and unconstitutional.

These examples offer a brief glimpse of what young people can bring to the fight for climate justice. They not only strengthen moral power, but their lived experience highlights their global climate leadership. Their activities draw our attention to the demands we should all be pushing for when it comes to political action on climate change. Their tenacity is a shining example of hope, particularly when geopolitical realities resulting from historical imbalances can seem too big to resist.

A Call for a Fossil Fuel Treaty

In 2015, the United Nations Framework Convention on Climate Change (UNFCCC) adopted the landmark Paris Agreement. This is the existing international legal framework governing states' responses to climate change.

The Paris Agreement requires countries to establish commitments to emissions reductions in line with the global goal of "holding the increase in the global average temperature to well below 2°C above pre-industrial levels and pursuing efforts to limit the temperature increase to 1.5°C above pre-industrial levels" (Art 2(1)(a)).[21] It also obliges countries to address climate adaptation, loss and damage, finance, technology transfer and capacity-building and transparency.

At its core, the Paris Agreement's mitigation obligations emphasise reduction of greenhouse gas emissions. Lower emissions can only be the result of restricted demand for fossil fuels, which should lead to a reduction in fossil fuel production. In reality, many states are still increasing their production of fossil fuels by more than double the amount that would have been compatible with keeping the temperature below a 1.5°C increase by 2030.[22] Fossil fuel production is *greater* than the emissions reduction commitments those states established in their national determined contributions (NDCs).

NDCs are central to the Paris Agreement as they illustrate what countries plan to do to reduce their emissions, and what actions they are taking to adapt to climate change. The Paris Agreement (Article 4, para 2) requires each state to arrange, communicate and sustain the NDCs that it aims to fulfill.[23]

Unfortunately, the Paris Agreement's parent treaty, the UNFCCC, does *not* set out targets or impose constraints on the production or use of coal, gas or oil. While the UNFCCC recognises the challenge faced by countries whose economies are dependent on fossil fuels, the lack of constraints on production and use (and even the absence of the term "fossil fuels" or the words "oil", "coal", or "gas" within the Paris Agreement text) means countries continue to find ways to maintain production. This only undermines the energy transition needed to meet their NDCs and, ultimately, the Paris Agreement's goals.

Despite the gravity of the situation, at the time of writing, fewer than 20% of the 195 parties to the Paris Agreement have submitted their NDC 3.0 commitments (and only 13 did so by the required deadline). Only a small number of these commitments are ambitious enough to keep global warming as close to 1.5°C as possible.

The last round of NDCs submitted in 2020 put us on a trajectory for a catastrophic rise in global warming of 2.5°C to 2.9°C. In 2024, fossil fuel usage and emissions reached a new record of 37.4 billion metric tonnes, a 0.8% increase on 2023 levels.[24] This disconnect between climate pledges and fossil fuel production is not just troubling, it is a clear indication that we are failing to meet our commitments, with many NDCs failing to address the root causes of the crisis. Fossil fuels including oil, coal and gas remain the primary driver of the climate emergency, accounting for a staggering 86% of CO_2 emissions over the past decade.[25]

We simply cannot afford to continue this way. With 2024 officially the warmest year on record and the first with average global temperatures more than 1.5°C above pre-industrial levels, we are edging closer to irreversible and catastrophic damage unless we radically shift our course.

Civil society actors and a group of progressive nation states have pushed for climate commitments under the UNFCCC and Paris Agreement frameworks that further emphasise the relationship between fossil fuels and climate change. These efforts have resulted in positive outcomes in recent years. In 2021, at COP26 in Glasgow, countries committed to "accelerating efforts towards the phase-out of unabated coal power and inefficient fossil fuel subsidies" (Decision 1/CMA.3, para 36).[26] At COP27 in Sharm El-Sheikh, states agreed to establish a transition work program, which has potential as an avenue for discussion on just transition options for fossil fuel dependent countries (Decision 1/CMA.4, para 53).[27] At the time of writing, however, this program is still in the process of being established. While it addresses scaling back fossil fuel production and use, it does not do so directly; nor does it provide any mechanism for implementation.

Countries, particularly those dependent on oil, gas and coal, should view their fossil fuel commitments as stepping stones towards gaining the financial and technical support so that they may transition to clean and sustainable energy. This transition should not be seen as a burden but rather as an opportunity for growth and innovation, enhancing the wellbeing of those communities affected by the shift. However, commitments in recent years still lack concrete measures for implementation. And at the time of writing, there remains a need for a clearer agenda item under the UNFCCC and Paris Agreement's decision-making bodies for negotiations on a framework or mechanism to guide the phasing out of fossil fuels.[28]

Under the UNFCCC's Mitigation Work Programme, countries sought for an inclusion of matters that are "urgently scaling up mitigation ambition and implementation" as referred to in paragraph 27 of Decision 1/CMA.3.[29] This includes phasing out fossil fuels — the best form of mitigation. However, during COP29 in Baku, countries called for the removal of references to fossil fuels in this context, which resulted in what would potentially have been a critical hook for discussions on the phasing out of fossil fuels being left without a dedicated home under the Mitigation Work Programme.

The third round of NDC submissions, or NDC 3.0, marks a crucial opportunity for countries to enhance their ambitions and fulfill their obligations under the Paris Agreement. Simply put, it's our chance to do better. Submissions were due in February 2025.

The Global Stocktake, held every five years, is a UNFCCC process established by the Paris Agreement to check in on the implementation of the Agreement and assess our global collective progress towards its long-term goals. Countries factor in the Global Stocktake's outcomes when developing their new NDCs.

At the Global Stocktake at COP28 in Dubai, countries acknowledged the need for "transitioning away from fossil fuels in energy systems, in a just, orderly and equitable manner, accelerating action in this critical decade, so as to achieve net zero by 2050 in keeping with the science" (Decision 1/CMA.5, para 28(d)).[30] This approach not only aligns with the objectives of the Paris Agreement but also sets a framework for an equitable and just transition from fossil fuel dependency.

NDCs should be based on equity, with developed countries phasing out fossil fuels quickly and in line with their greater capacity to do so, while also providing finance, technology and capacity-building support to ensure developing countries will benefit from the transition. Individual country NDCs should reflect this principle of equity in their commitments. It is imperative that updated NDCs directly address the primary cause of the problem — fossil fuel production and use. The Pact for the Future adopted by the UN General Assembly (UNGA) in September 2024 further cements the COP28 language relating to fossil fuels, reconfirming countries' obligations to transition away from fossil fuels and demonstrating that fossil fuels are one of the key challenges on the multilateral agenda.[31]

The relationship between fossil fuels and climate change cannot be ignored or omitted; it is an indispensable part of the context for countries' climate change commitments. Global warming is caused by the increasing accumulation of greenhouse gases in the atmosphere. The overwhelming driver of these GHG emissions is fossil fuel combustion and industrial processes. Ignoring fossil fuel production is at the heart of the failure to adequately address the climate emergency. This is despite the fact that the role of fossil fuels in driving the emergency is indisputable.

What the UNFCCC and the Paris Agreement provide is a framework to address the crisis, including the mitigation of further climate change as well as adaptation to its effects. But while countries can include fossil fuel supply-side measures in their NDCs, they are not spelt out as an explicit requirement in current frameworks. In these treaties, there is a need to directly address ongoing production of the substances that are responsible for climate change.

In 2024, the International Tribunal for the Law of the Sea Advisory Opinion (ITLOS) on climate change found the Paris Agreement and UNFCCC do not adequately "cover the field", and that climate-related obligations are also derived from other international treaty instruments and customary international law.[32] ITLOS clarified that, under UNCLOS, states have separate and stringent obligations to protect and preserve the marine environment from the catastrophic effects of climate change.

It's extraordinary that it took us 28 years of negotiations within the UNFCCC framework before we were able to reach a point where fossil fuels were mentioned in the COP outcome document. It's as absurd as Alcoholics Anonymous holding 28 years of conferences but never mentioning the word "alcohol". I attribute this to the fact that at most COPs the largest delegation is usually from the fossil fuel industry. At COP30 in Brazil 1600 lobbyists from the fossil fuel sector were present. Put differently, for every 25 delegates one was from the fossil fuel industry: imagine if the largest delegation at an Alcoholics Anonymous conference were the alcohol industry! Fossil fuel lobbyists have managed to divert our attention from the root cause of the problem.

In international law, it is rare that a global issue is entirely regulated or addressed through one treaty. Governance tends to evolve over time, especially as the understanding of the problem changes, along with the political will. And as has been the case over the past 30 or so years, our governance framework on climate change needs to change. Urgently.

Climate change is currently overseen by a range of legal instruments. These include the UNFCCC and its subsidiary instruments the Kyoto Protocol and the Paris Agreement. There is also a range of other treaties and "soft-law" instruments such as the Montreal Protocol (1995) and its Kigali Amendment (2016); the Intergovernmental Panel on Climate Change (IPCC) and its governing structures; multilateral development banks and related agreements; Just Energy Transition Partnerships; bilateral agreements; clubs of countries (for example, the G20 and the G7); initiatives such as the Beyond Oil and Gas Alliance and Powering Past Coal Alliance; the Sendai Framework for Disaster Risk Reduction; the United Nations' Sustainable Development Goals; regional insurance mechanisms, and others.[33] As noted earlier, a growing body of international law is beginning to recognise that countries have obligations with respect to limiting greenhouse gas emissions, and that these obligations derive not only from the UNFCCC and the Paris Agreement.

On the frontlines, resistance continues to grow. With the collective goal of creating a comprehensive new international mechanism to tackle the root causes of the climate crisis, the leadership of nations like Vanuatu and Tuvalu has brought together other forward-thinking countries in a "coalition of the willing". The new international mechanism that these first-mover island states are hoping to create is an ambitious and bold idea called the Fossil Fuel Non-Proliferation Treaty (also known as the Fossil Fuel Treaty).

Vanuatu and Tuvalu are particularly vulnerable to the effects of climate change. Tuvalu is an archipelago of nine islands, with two of these already disappearing due to rising sea levels and erosion. Most of Tuvalu's landmass is less than 3 metres above sea level. In recent years, rising tides have salted the soil and the groundwater and eroded the shorelines. Vanuatu is vulnerable due its position in the "ring of fire" which means volcanic activity and earthquakes are not uncommon. It also regularly experiences cyclones and extreme rainfall.

Scientists have warned that Pacific Islands such as these could be uninhabitable in 50 years. But they are refusing to give up hope. Vanuatu and Tuvalu were among the first countries to call for a Fossil Fuel Treaty — a binding agreement to align oil, gas and coal production with a global carbon budget. Decades ago, we should have stopped fossil fuel production and use. But we did not. Whatever good we do in terms of increasing renewable energy output — all of which needs to scale up exponentially — does not solve the problem if we continue to produce and burn fossil fuels.

Attending COPs since 2008, many of my colleagues and I have repeatedly asked for a fair, ambitious and binding (FAB) deal. Sadly, year in, year out we come away disappointed with FLAB outcomes (full of loopholes and BS). Imagine we came home from work one day and found the bath had overflowed because we left the tap running. Would we start mopping the floor, or would we first turn off the tap? The fossil fuel industry has worked hard to shift our focus away from "turning off the tap" to selling us "super-absorbent" mops and pretending as if this were climate action.

Despite not getting all we have wanted, we have worked hard to achieve some important victories in the UNFCCC climate negotiations. We continue to support the Paris Agreement, but it is now clear that such actions must be augmented by stronger measures — a binding Fossil Fuel Non-Proliferation Treaty.

Such a treaty aims to complement the existing UNFCCC mechanisms, including the Work

Programme on just transition established at COP27, by contributing to a clear plan towards a just transition from fossil fuels through two important initiatives. First, we must enforce the obligations relating to the phasing out of fossil fuels that support the effective fulfilment of the letter and spirit of the Paris Agreement and the UNFCCC. Second, we must establish coordinated measures at a multilateral level to fill the policy gap on fossil fuel supply.

The proposed Fossil Fuel Treaty includes the following provisions:

- Centre the need for a just and equitable transition away from fossil fuels by addressing the structural economic challenges that lock many countries into continued fossil fuel dependence;
- End the expansion of new fossil fuel extraction projects;
- Require an equitable phase-out of existing fossil fuel extraction projects on the basis of historical responsibilities and the principle of common but differentiated responsibilities and respective capabilities (CBDR-RC) in

light of different national circumstances, with developed countries moving first and fastest;

- Include the provision of finance, technology and capacity-building support to enable those countries that are locked into continued fossil fuel dependence to transition to alternative economic development pathways;
- Encourage just transition measures to ensure fossil fuel dependent workers and communities are supported through the transition;
- Create incentive mechanisms to make it attractive for countries to participate in the Treaty, and impose costs on fossil fuel producers that do not ratify the Treaty;
- Establish transparency measures so countries are required to report on their fossil fuel production and other activities such as public finance support for fossil fuels; and
- Clarify the relationship between the Treaty and the broader international trade regime and Investor State Dispute Settlement regime.

While the UNFCCC and Paris Agreement do not directly regulate fossil fuel production and supply, they contain provisions that align with a just and equitable phase-out. The Fossil Fuel Treaty aims to complement these existing frameworks by focusing on the supply side.

The hope is that as obligations set out in the Treaty come to fruition, countries will not only be better placed to limit warming, but also have the means to implement the necessary changes.

A Fossil Fuel Treaty complements the existing legal instruments by addressing regulatory gaps without duplicating measures. The UNFCCC and Paris Agreement have near universal participation, while the Fossil Fuel Treaty would likely involve fewer member states, at least initially. For states that are party to the UNFCCC or Paris Agreement but not the Fossil Fuel Treaty, the Fossil Fuel Treaty would not affect their other obligations.

By establishing obligations based on fossil fuel supply, the Fossil Fuel Treaty will help to implement the temperature limit advocated by the Paris Agreement.

Furthermore, the Fossil Fuel Treaty offers a basis for applying the principle of common but differentiated responsibilities and respective capabilities (CBDR-RC) in relation to fossil fuel dependence and economic diversification. CBDR-RC means that states with smaller GDP and fewer resources, along with smaller per capita pollution, are not required to take as much or as expensive action as richer states. This is compatible with Article 4 of the UNFCCC, which provides that parties shall take into consideration the situation of developing country parties in particular, including those with economies highly dependent on income generated from fossil fuels.[34]

The UNFCCC and the Paris Agreement recognise the challenges associated with a just transition for fossil fuel dependent developing countries. In order to meet the goals of the Paris Agreement, we need international cooperation to stop the expansion of fossil fuel production and use and to manage a just global transition away from coal, oil and gas in a manner that is both fast and fair, so that no worker, community or country is left behind.

The Treaty also aims to complement other strategies such as divestment, debt relief and fossil fuel bans as well as the work being advanced by organisations such as the Beyond Oil and Gas Alliance and the Power Past Coal Alliance.

Momentum is building behind the Treaty. Academics, scientists, youth activists, health professionals, faith institutions and millions of citizens globally have come together in support of it. This big, bold idea is appealing in part because it is commensurate with the scale of the crisis we face. The Treaty builds on decades of calls and campaigns by governments, civil society, Indigenous, grassroots and other leaders — particularly from the Global South.

In 2015, officials and civil society leaders in the Pacific put forward a bold proposal. The 2015 Suva Declaration on Climate Change, issued from the Pacific Islands Development Forum Third Annual Summit held in Suva, Fiji, called for "a new global dialogue on the implementation of an international moratorium on the development and expansion of fossil fuel extracting industries, particularly the construction of new coal mines, as an urgent step towards decarbonising the global economy".[35]

The following year, after a summit in the Solomon Islands, 14 Pacific Island nations came together to discuss the world's first treaty to ban new coal mining and embrace the 1.5°C goal set at the Paris climate talks.

In 2017, the Least Developed Countries (LDC) group made a joint closing statement at COP23, chaired by Fiji and held in Bonn, in which they stressed the need for "an increase in ambition by all countries to put us on track to limit the global temperature increase to 1.5 degrees Celcius by strengthening our national contributions, managing a phase-out of fossil fuels, promoting renewable energy and implementing the most ambitious climate action".[36]

Civil society leaders have also mobilised for a global phase-out. This led to the Lofoten Declaration, written in 2017 at a gathering in the Lofoten Islands, Norway, which recognised the urgent need to stop the expansion of the oil and gas industries in order to achieve the Paris Agreement goals. It also called for action to be taken first by countries who have benefited the most from fossil fuel extraction — and having a historical responsibility — but being also the best positioned to take action for a just global transition. The declaration stated, "It is the urgent responsibility and moral obligation of wealthy fossil fuel producers to lead in putting an end to fossil fuel development and to manage the decline of existing production."[37]

During the discussions around the Lofoten Declaration, some participants made analogies to weapons treaties with landmines and nuclear ban treaties. There is much to admire in the way the peace and disarmament movements have campaigned, especially the International Campaign to Abolish Nuclear Weapons (ICAN). Founded in Melbourne in 2007, ICAN coordinated civil society and grassroots efforts from around the world to stop the proliferation of nuclear weapons.[38] Treating fossil fuels in a similar way has been advocated by prominent scholars, notably Peter Newell and Andrew Simms in an article published in 2019.[39]

The Fossil Fuel Treaty draws on the example of many successful agreements before it, including the Mine Ban Treaty. In the simplest terms, the Mine Ban Treaty showed us that ambitious countries could come together to negotiate a treaty outside of the UN system. Once established, they took the treaty to the UN to ratify it. The United States, China and Russia did not sign. But despite that, the manufacture, distribution and deployment of landmines came to a virtual standstill. The Fossil Fuel Treaty hopes to do the same.

There is no doubt we need consensus on the urgency of transitioning away from fossil fuels. Yet such consensus is not only based on shaky geopolitical ground but is also affected — and fundamentally hampered — by powerful fossil fuel interests. What we can see from the International Energy Agency's tracking is that investment in renewable energy is increasing — but at the same time, investment in oil, gas and coal is up since 2020.[40]

Two-thirds of the global increase in energy demand in 2023 was met by fossil fuels. It should be no surprise that energy-related CO_2 emissions reached a record high. A transition *is* happening, but the world cannot meet the goals of the Paris Agreement without an urgent step change.

—

In 2023, ministers and officials from a bloc of six Pacific Island nations — Vanuatu, Tuvalu, Tonga, Fiji, Niue and the Solomon Islands — agreed on a resolution called the Port Vila Call for a Just Transition to a Fossil Fuel Free Pacific.[41]

It proclaimed the need for a Fossil Fuel Non-Proliferation Treaty and sparked the creation of a global alliance to work on its creation.

To discuss securing a negotiating mandate for the Treaty and how to bring more countries on board, in 2024, the first ministerial meeting of the bloc of nation states involved in the Treaty was convened in the lead-up to the 4th International Conference on Small Island Developing States (SIDS4). In collaboration with the governments of Tuvalu and Vanuatu, the meeting was hosted by Antigua and Barbuda, the first Caribbean country to join the bloc.

In 2024, amid a groundswell of international support, Pacific civil society organisations joined by faith, youth and Indigenous communities launched the Naiuli Declaration for a Fossil Fuel Non-Proliferation Treaty.[42] Marking a significant milestone in the global movement to tackle climate change, it was the first declaration of support for the Treaty from the region's civil society organisations. The declaration, serving as the "North Star" for climate action, demanded the highest level of ambition not only from Pacific Island leaders but from all governments around the world. It reaffirmed the collective commitment of Pacific Islands civil society to drive the ambition of the Treaty.

Despite this progress, the fossil fuel economy continues to present substantial structural and political challenges. Various multilateral fora — including the Plastics Treaty Negotiations, the UNFCCC, the Summit of the Future, and United Nations General Assembly (UNGA) resolutions — face obstacles to achieving specific and implementable steps forward on fossil fuels. The geopolitical context is further complicated by some nations increasingly opposing or withdrawing from multilateral processes altogether. However, such obstacles also create opportunities to transform international environmental governance. There is growing openness in the broader international community to consider alternative approaches.

The biggest threats of our time require connection, cooperation and trust — that is why they are so often addressed by conferences and meetings. We've seen this happen with past threats that brought interested parties together with a goal of setting a vision and agreeing to next steps. It is this sense of community action and solidarity that brought together the people of Lismore in 2014 to establish one of the largest anti-fracking movements in Australia, and the students of Vanuatu to take their climate change fight to the world's highest international court.

Concentrating on the transition as one element of current complex and wide-ranging negotiations has diluted focus on the root problem, allowed some participants to be obstructionist, and stymied the fruitful discussion of solutions. Yet from these negotiations, it is clear that there is political support around the world to advance a just and equitable transition.

The countries pushing for a Fossil Fuel Treaty have suggested holding a series of diplomatic conferences from 2026 onwards with the goal of fostering international cooperation for a just transition. During the UNGA in September 2025, the government of Colombia announced its plan to host the First International Conference for the Phase-Out of Fossil Fuels in April 2026. This landmark conference aims to provide a global platform for countries to cooperate.

The announcement marked the first political step towards the conference launch, which then unfolded at COP30 in November 2025 in Belém. Colombia, with the Netherlands, announced they would be co-hosting the Conference on 28–29 April 2026 in the port city of Santa Marta, Colombia, which plays a significant role in coal exports. Hosting this summit in a major coal port, in the world's fifth-largest coal producer, sends the message that fossil fuel dependent nations who want to end their dependence on oil, gas and coal extraction can — but that doing so fairly requires unprecedented international cooperation if the just transition is to ensure no one is left behind. The conference would advance the development of the Treaty, building on examples of previous diplomatic summits that have led to increased international cooperation and treaty negotiations aiming to address major global threats.

Political leaders who side with fossil fuel interests undermine international cooperation and delay climate action, fostering scepticism and discrediting multilateral efforts. Their actions are poisoning our air, our waters, our lands, our ecosystems, our people and our politics. They are spreading lies and false solutions and backing away from global commitments. The fossil fuel industry knew for decades that their products would burn the planet, but they buried the science, bribed politicians and tried to make us believe there was no alternative. They fattened themselves with record profits — in 2022 alone, the fossil fuel industry recorded a US$4 trillion net income — while fossil fuel subsidies reached US$7 trillion. They let the Global South drown in debt and rising seas, demanding that poor nations drill more oil and mine more coal, just to pay interest on loans that enrich the few.

Failing to develop ambitious and binding frameworks that regulate the causes of the climate crisis means failing to uphold the right to life and self-determination, the right to adequate food, the right to water, the right to health, and the right to adequate housing of communities in vulnerable, coastal states and other groups that are disproportionately affected. Such a failure is something we can ill afford.

Currents of Solidarity

When I was a young activist, I heard the Native American saying, "Only when the last tree has been cut down, the last fish been caught, and the last stream poisoned, will we realise we cannot eat money."

My struggle against injustice started but did not end with the apartheid era. Having tried to bring about positive change in the world for the last 45 years, I am forced to admit that activism, in its current form, is failing. Gross social and economic inequalities are on the rise, the climate crisis threatens humanity's survival, and military and civil conflicts around the world — not least the horrific genocide in Palestine — are increasing. More than ever, there is a need for citizens to hold power to account, but I believe we have to find new, more effective ways to do so.

Recent armed invasions and conflicts have exposed the rot at the heart of our systems: in the name of greed, territories around the world are illegally occupied, populations are displaced, and injustices are worsening. The simultaneous crises of war, debt distress and climate breakdown are not isolated — they are symptoms of the same extractive logic. Fuelling all of them is the greatest threat of our time: fossil fuels, "the very lifeblood of powering conflicts".[43] But these interconnected crises also point to the way forward: ending our dependence on fossil fuels isn't just about avoiding disasters — it's about building energy, food and economic security and peace through policies that invest in the interests of communities and the global majority, not just a small fraction of elites. Future wars will not just be fought over oil, they will be fought over water. Water is the most critical resource that we have on our planet but for decades we have been irresponsibly harming it.

The links between conflict and fossil fuels are mediated by geopolitical networks and global and national economic and financial systems. The Fossil Fuel Treaty aims to challenge the structures and systems that have led to the situation in which we now find ourselves. Fossil fuels are implicated in civil wars and separatist movements, as well as in human rights violations and systemic violence. Feminist activists have repeatedly pointed out that a narrow interpretation of violence is a major challenge to recognising the fact that violence operates on a peacetime–wartime continuum and has roots in existing inequalities and harmful gender norms.

The Fossil Fuel Treaty would advocate for cooperation, disarmament, trust-building and ecological diplomacy to prevent war, militarisation and conflict, including over critical minerals. It will reform policies and practices of international financial institutions, moving them away from promotion of harmful and regressive austerity and privatisation measures. Dedicated debt cancellation mechanisms at the UN level and climate and colonial reparations will ensure the transfer of funds and sound technologies to the Global South.

Relying on fossil fuels today is akin to building our future on sinking sand. In regions such as the North Sea, Mexico and the United States, oil production has already peaked. The cheap, easy-to-access reserves are gone. What's left is dirtier, harder to reach and more expensive to extract. But rather than accepting this reality, fossil fuel companies are doing everything they can to prolong this outdated system — drilling to the last drop, lobbying to delay the transition, and locking us into more pipelines and infrastructure we don't need. None of this is about energy security; it's about protecting profits.

Fossil fuels are a finite, unstable resource, incompatible with a safe future. Moving beyond them isn't just good for the climate — it's the only path that makes economic and strategic sense. Yet there is currently insufficient international cooperation to manage their equitable phase-out. Instead, many governments continue to approve extraction plans that make a mockery of climate goals. The United Nations Environment Programme's (UNEP) 2023 Production Gap Report warned that countries plan to extract fossil fuels at levels that will result in more than double the emissions by 2030 than the 1.5°C limit allows.[44]

The social contract between citizens and governments is broken and needs urgent renewal. For those of us who believe in the possibility of change, we must finish the job we started. Were it not for progressive activism and the sacrifices that have been made by many in previous generations, there would be an even worse crisis than we currently find ourselves in.

In many ways, my generation has failed one of our era's greatest challenges. We now need to listen and respond to the voices of young people. Humanity is on a dangerous path, and it will be up to the next generation to steer us in a new direction. It will not be easy. We will need to work out how to connect our different struggles and develop a new understanding of the relationship between people and their governments: in essence, we will need a new eco-social contract. Too many young people have reached the point of desperation, questioning their very worth. But pessimism is a luxury we cannot afford. The pessimism that emerges from our analysis, our lived experience and our observations can be overcome by the optimism of our thought, our action, our creativity, our courage, and our sense of humanity.

It is critical for us to urgently address the problems of eco-anxiety and the global mental health crisis. We need to increase public awareness and involvement exponentially. And we need to adopt an approach that has multiple ways in which people can help. We need to do all this for two reasons. First, if you want to get our business and political leaders to move as fast as we need them to, we need public mobilisation on a scale never seen before. Second, we need to recognise that one antidote to the global mental health crisis is not pessimism, but participation.

Much of the focus around ecological issues is shifting towards climate justice. Today, environmental movements commonly blend socio-political and socio-economic themes as the underpinning for their actions.[45] While we support these changes, we have to address the reasons why we're still facing setbacks on climate activism and why we're seeing a rise in racism and fascism. We have thus far not addressed these issues in a truly intersectional way. We therefore need to turbocharge intersectionality, in our thinking and our practice.

And that's why people like me are part of the problem. For far too long we aimed all our narratives at the brain and ignored the heart, the body and the soul. We're now seeing the emergence of a new global movement, aligned to the values of a Fossil Fuel Treaty, but that also seeks to promote a concept known as "artivism". We have been promoting big ideas, technical vernacular and complex theoretical concepts for decades. We now need to acknowledge that while we have material needs, we are also spiritual beings. We must appeal to people's hearts as well as their heads, bringing together art, culture and activism in a way that engages people's deepest impulses of love, justice and freedom.

Artivism is for people who don't necessarily have the education or the time to wade through endless technical documents. Often, when climate activists talk about addressing the energy transition, we use arcane scientific jargon. We discuss policies that are too complicated to articulate in simple terms. We use so many acronyms that we risk drowning people in an alphabet soup. In this essay alone, I've mentioned EEZs, UNGA, UNEP, UNCLOS, the UNFCCC and GHGs. Usage of this nature has become second nature to academics and activists, but it's a foreign language to most laypeople.

Historically, the dissemination (particularly in and from the Global North) of information about the climate crisis has been framed in inaccessible ways — the documents are often highly technical and lack an intersectional justice lens.[46] This can lead to continued oppression and maintaining the status quo.[47]

While working as an activist with Greenpeace, I recall mainstream media sources regularly portraying peaceful demonstrations by environmentalists as disruptive, or even violent. This was deeply problematic, but those media companies were able to use their position of power to control the narrative.[48] While the climate science was clear, the power of spinning the truth was not. The layperson would not have been able to understand what interpretation of the science motivated activists to protest or demonstrate in the first place. When the legacy media filed their reports, the urgency of taking action to address the crisis was lost. It was suggested that the protesters, aided and abetted by trouble-making scientists, were just ruining businesses and disrupting ordinary people's lives.

As young activists come to terms with the ecological crisis into which they have been born but never asked for, they are driving deeper conversations about the pathway forward. Their raw emotions are part of what captures the imaginations of ordinary people. The Fridays for Future movement, begun by

Greta Thunberg in Sweden in 2018, has helped personalise climate messaging, taking the concerns of students to the global stage with the help of digital platforms.[49]

Today, tackling the climate crisis is no longer about just holding up traffic or waving placards outside an office building. With greater access to information, social and environmental movements have more democratic platforms that include diverse voices and engage instantly and globally, allowing civil society and vulnerable communities to tell their own stories first-hand. Thanks to the internet, the youth climate movement is reminding us all what needs to be done to protect what we love in real time.

—

Democratising activism through art is not only the province of the climate movement; it was an essential part of the Civil Rights and Black Lives Matter movements in the United States as well.[50] Artistic expression allowed historically oppressed groups to convey the depth of their lived experience and challenge the dominant narratives by bringing their own perspectives and sensemaking to the foreground.

This is not a new phenomenon. Movements that have changed history have long been carried by art, song and story. In the anti-apartheid struggle, we sang our courage before we could live it. Today, I see the same spirit in young Pacific Island artists painting their islands' stories, and in First Nations' poets transforming their grief into resistance. Art is not merely decoration — it is declaration. It gives us a language for what statistics cannot communicate and hope for what politics cannot deliver.

As a form of resistance against colonial extractivism, Indigenous groups from the Brazilian Amazon have used art to illuminate their struggles.[51] They challenged the notion that their natural resources were something to be exploited, reminding the world of their relationship with nature and contesting the idea that Mother Earth is only an economic resource from which one can profit. This "artivism" not only emphasised how resisting colonial extractivism was best for their community's wellbeing, but how the stories of Indigenous people are vital for sustaining our interconnected ecosystems' wellbeing too.

Artivism frames themes of social injustice that can evoke pain and grief.[52] But art and culture can also promote hope and beauty in order to drive change. Similarly, when we want to motivate large groups of people, we must not forget the role that faith can play. Published in May 2015, the Catholic Laudato Si' is an encyclical of the late Pope Francis that focuses on care for the natural environment and all people.[53] Importantly, the publication was subtitled "on care for our common home". Pope Francis not only criticised consumerism and irresponsible economic development, but he also called for a multifaith, inclusive co-existence for a "swift and unified global" response to environmental degradation and global warming.

While the Pope is just one world leader, Christianity remains one of the largest faith groups in the world with some 73% of the world's Catholics living in the Global South. Having a religious leader so adamantly call out inequality and poverty — and link it to the climate crisis — was as necessary in 2015 as it is now.

In October 2025 I addressed the tenth anniversary of the Laudato Si' which was opened by Pope Francis's successor, Pope Leo XIV, in Rome. Pope Leo embraced Pope Francis's environmental legacy and seconded his predecessor's calls to continue pressuring governments to establish and develop tougher standards to mitigate the effects of climate change. The Pope's actions amplified the call of Indigenous groups who were in attendance, including many representatives from the Pacific.

—

Harnessing the power of art, culture, poetry, music and faith to create change and compelling narratives, and weaving together traditional forms with modern, digital storytelling, This Is Our Home: Pacific Artists for Climate Justice unites Indigenous artists and storytellers from across the Pacific to advocate for climate action and a fossil fuel free future.[54] This Is Our Home has performed on global stages, including with the British band Coldplay in Lyon, France, in June 2024.

Stories, oral traditions, art, culture and music have been the tools with which Pacific Island peoples have passed down their knowledge, histories and heritage for millennia. These tools represent a central part of the many cultures that populate the Pacific and are the archives of their ancestors. The arts have taught Pacific Islanders about the world around them and the histories of their people. The arts have taught them about the struggles they faced, from the early 1900s freedom songs of Samoa's independence leaders, to the songs of sorrow from communities in Vanuatu and Tokelau, as they endured the brutality of slavery at the hands of Western colonial empires. Art, music and storytelling are the collective memory of these communities.

Exploring how Pacific Islands values, faith and cultures have fostered innovation and resilience, This Is Our Home brings the current battles that Pacific communities confront into popular culture. Projects like this break the control of powerful states over political discourse with something even more powerful: emotive, human-centered stories that move hearts and minds into action.

My late son, Rikhado, was an artist. One of the many important things I learnt from Riky was the unsurpassed power of art and culture to move us and motivate us in truly transformative ways. Riky made music that resonated with young people around the world; he inspired them to dream big and believe in themselves. Through his music, Riky had an ability to reach people that went far beyond anything his mother or I could hope to achieve through activism.

Riky and I often spoke about his potential to be a force for good in society. We spoke of setting up a foundation to support young artists in particular. Riky taught me that activism must change. Upon his passing, our family set up the Riky Rick Foundation for the Promotion of Artivism. This led to the development of the Global Artivism movement, which brings together artists, activists and allies across the globe to build the power of artists in social movements, shift culture, and mobilise for global justice and a healthy planet. At an annual conference, the movement creates space where artivists can connect, collaborate and thrive, ensuring cultural power works towards political and social transformation.

Today, it is these young climate activists and artists who are providing an intersectional lens on climate action. They are using artivism to rewrite their epilogue of the climate emergency tale, from one of devastation and potential apocalypse, to a liveable future.

What We Owe the Water

My story started decades ago in a South African school where water came from a single tap under a giant fig tree. I knew from a young age that this precious substance was something that we desperately needed but could easily run out of.

In my childhood, the name Nelson Mandela was whispered as a cautionary tale about the dangers of political activism, lest we end up jailed alongside him on Robben Island, surrounded by shark-infested waters. My story with water was political from very early on. And while my story has shifted many times over, the story of water has not. Water can nourish us and sustain us, as quickly as it can flood our homes and take it all away.

Nowhere is this more apparent than in the Pacific Islands.

Pacific Island nations bear almost no historical responsibility for our current climate crisis yet are acutely vulnerable to its catastrophic effects. Pacific Island governments' leadership for limiting warming must therefore be cemented through a joint call for an equitable global phase-out of fossil fuels and for a just transition. Countries like Vanuatu and Tuvalu have refused to accept what they called a "death sentence". They stood up and spoke out. They said that this was not a crisis. It was a crime. The theft of a safe and stable environment. The theft of sovereignty by an industry that disregards borders and discards people. The theft of the future of millions of us, our children and generations to come.

An ambitious, binding Fossil Fuel Treaty is an opportunity to set a high-water mark for action, while supporting a just and equitable global transition that is not only aligned with the goals of the UNFCCC and the Paris Agreement, but that will contribute towards a healthier, safer and more prosperous future for all.

Five years ago, the proposal for such a treaty was just an idea, a glimmer of hope in tumultuous times. Today, thanks to the support of thousands of organisations and institutions, more than a million people, and a growing group of (at the time of writing) 18 forward-thinking nations that started in the Pacific, it is a catalyst for real change.

The current movement is proof that collaboration is the only way to dismantle old systems. It is the only way to give people faith that there is a way forward. And it is the only way to build a new world. Not the "business as usual" world as we have always known it. But one where governments and civil society break stalemates together, ensuring that the transition is not some sort of "green colonialism" replicating the same old extractive practices, but a true people-centred economy; decentralised and democratically governed and owned by communities, not corporations.

Political focus on the concept of "just transition" has increased in recent years, as has the uptake and installation of renewable energy options. Yet the extraction, transport and combustion of fossil fuels has continued to expand, pushing carbon emissions to their highest levels in human history. This growth has been underwritten by increases in fossil fuel subsidies, despite longstanding commitments to end them.

In 2025, renewable energy is cheaper than fossil fuels in almost every country. Clean energy investments are greater than fossil fuel investments by a factor of two. In many countries, 90% of the growth in new energy sources comes from solar and wind. And yet the potential of renewable energy is held back because there is no unified plan to manage the transition away from coal, oil and gas.

As the world shifts in ways once considered unthinkable, and as we watch long-established alliances, policies and norms vacated and abandoned, we have an opportunity to push for the world we want and need. We have the opportunity to chart a new course — but this requires a courageous global response. We do not have time for backtracking or half-measures. Without decisive, meaningful action to halt the expansion of oil, gas and coal — and to pursue a just and equitable transition — we risk a future that is not just bleak for the environment but bleak for global development, peace and security.

We've seen crises unite the world before: the COVID-19 pandemic spurred global cooperation; while international treaties have phased out landmines, banned the exponential proliferation of nuclear weapons, and saved the ozone.

These victories proved that first-mover governments can change the course of history, especially when done in coalition with civil society, the private sector and other concerned parties. What we need now is the political will to fight the fossil fuel giants and their allies in power that are preventing progress. It is inevitable that they will keep pushing back, funding their marketing machine, spreading disinformation and paying lobbyists. But we know better. We are seeing the alternatives bloom, and we are done choosing the path of destruction.

The historic leadership coming from Pacific Island nations should instil in us all a deeper understanding of our relationship with water, the most abundant resource on our planet, particularly as it relates to tackling the deepest roots of injustice. To harm water is to harm life itself. The climate crisis is not only ecological — it is spiritual. We have broken our covenant with the living systems that sustain us, and it is time to restore that relationship with humility and gratitude.

The Pacific has led the call for climate justice for decades — just as generations of Pacific

Islanders stewarded the land and water inherited from their ancestors for thousands of years. Pacific Islanders remind us that the type of ancestors we one day will become will depend on what we do today, how we act now.

This is a story about moral courage, solidarity and the urgent need to recognise and honour the water that sustains all life. Because in the end, we do not inherit the Earth and its waters from our ancestors. We borrow them from our children.

When the water calls in our debt, we must answer not with fear but with fairness. We can still choose to pay it back in courage — by turning away from fossil fuels, by protecting every river and reef, and by standing together, Pacific and Australian, rich and poor, ancestor and child. The tides are rising, yes — but so are we.

About the author

Kumi Naidoo is a South African human rights and environmental justice activist and author. He is currently the President of the Fossil Fuel Non-Proliferation Treaty. Formerly, he was Secretary-General of Amnesty International (2018–2020) and Executive Director of Greenpeace International (2009–2015).

Endnotes

1 Alexeyeff and McDonnell (2018) "Whose paradise? Encounter, exchange, and exploitation", *The Contemporary Pacific*, 30(2), 269–295

2 Bones and Ferns (2022) "Pacific Nation or Neighbour: Australia's Relationship with New Zealand, Papua New Guinea, and the Pacific", *Australia on the World Stage*, pp 171–184

3 Patel (2024) "Aftermath of Nuclear Testing in the Pacific Islands", *JCO Global Oncology*, 10, e2400455

4 Maclellan (2017) Grappling with the bomb: Britain's Pacific H-Bomb Tests, Introduction

5 Guterres (2021) "The IPCC Report is a code red for humanity", United Nations, https://unric.org/en/guterres-the-ipcc-report-is-a-code-red-for-humanity/

6 *The Pacific Climate Warriors Declaration on Climate Change* (2017), https://act.350.org/sign/pcw-declaration?r=AU&c=OC

7 *Special Report on the Ocean and Cryosphere in a Changing Climate* (2016), https://www.ipcc.ch/srocc/

8 *Uncommon Wealth: Fossil Fuel Expansion in The Commonwealth Dominated by Three Wealthy Countries* (2024), FossilFuelTreaty.org

9 Fossil Fuel Treaty (2025) *Exporting Harm: The Climate Toll of Australia's Fossil Fuel*

Expansion, https://static1.squarespace.com/static/5dd3cc5b7fd99372fbb04561/t/67d1d4c8136e9a0ee930bf01/1741804775133/Australia+Report.pdf

10 King (2023), *Resources Statement to Parliament*, https://www.minister.industry.gov.au/ministers/king/speeches/resources-statement-parliament

11 King (2025), https://www.aph.gov.au/About_Parliament/Parliamentary_departments/Parliamentary_Library/Research/Policy_Briefs/2025-26/ClimatesecurityinthePacificregion

12 Engelbrecht et al. (2025) "Extreme event attribution using km-scale simulations reveals the pronounced role of climate change in the Durban floods", *Communications Earth & Environment*, https://doi.org/10.1038/s43247-025-02460-5

13 Matovu (2024) "Relevance of the high seas: Treaty towards Ocean sustainability targets in the Global South", *KMI International Journal of Maritime Affairs and Fisheries*, 16(1), 21–54

14 Request for an Advisory Opinion submitted by the Commission of Small Island States on Climate Change and International Law (Request for Advisory Opinion submitted to the Tribunal), Advisory Opinion of 21 May 2024, International Tribunal of the Law of the Sea, Case No. 31

15 Matovu (2024)

16 Matovu (2024)

17 Ben Mariem (2025) "UN welcomes ratification of ocean biodiversity protection agreement", https://www.jurist.org/news/2025/09/un-welcomes-ratification-of-ocean-biodiversity-protection-agreement/

18 Matovu (2024)

19 Stoutenburg (2013) "When Do States Disappear? Thresholds of Effective Statehood and the Continued Recognition of 'Deterritorialized' Island States", *Threatened Island Nations: Legal Implications of Rising Seas and a Changing Climate*, 57, 68

20 ICJ (2025) "Summary of the Advisory Opinion of 23 July 2025", https://www.icj-cij.org/node/205627

21 IPCC (2018) "Summary for Policymakers", *Global Warming of 1.5°C. An IPCC Special Report on the Impacts of Global Warming of 1.5°C above Pre-Industrial Levels and Related Global Greenhouse Gas Emission Pathways, in the Context of Strengthening the Global Response to the Threat of Climate Change, Sustainable Development, and Efforts to Eradicate Poverty*, World Meteorological Organization, http://www.ipcc.ch/report/sr15/; Decision 1/CMA.5, 4–5, 25–28

22 Stockholm Environment Institute et al. (2023) "The Production Gap: Phasing down or Phasing up? Top Fossil Fuel Producers Plan Even More Extraction despite Climate Promises", https://doi.org/10.51414/sei2023.050

23 *Nationally Determined Contributions (NDCs) The Paris Agreement and NDCs* (2015) shttps://unfccc.int/process-and-meetings/the-paris-agreement/nationally-determined-contributions-ndcs

24 Canadell et al. (2024) *Global carbon emissions inch upwards in 2024 despite progress on EVs, renewables and deforestation*, CSIRO, https://www.csiro.au/en/news/All/Articles/2024/November/Global-carbon-emissions-up-2024

25 Janzwood and Harrison (2023) "The political economy of fossil fuel production in the Post-Paris

Era: Critically evaluating Nationally Determined Contributions", *Energy Research & Social Science*, 102, 103095

26 UNFCCC (2021) "Draft CMA decision proposed by the president", https://unfccc.int/sites/default/files/resource/Overarching_decision_1-CMA-3_1.pdf

27 UNFCCC (2018) "Further guidance in relation to the mitigation section of decision 1/CP.21", https://unfccc.int/sites/default/files/resource/4-CMA.1_English.pdf

28 The Conference of the Parties to the UNFCCC or COP, and the Conference of the Parties serving as the meeting of the Parties to the Paris Agreement or CMA, respectively.

29 UNFCCC (2021) "Draft CMA decision proposed by the president"

30 UNFCCC (2023) "Outcome of the first global stocktake", https://unfccc.int/documents/636608

31 UNRIC (2024) "Pact for the Future: A Vision for Global Collaboration" https://unric.org/en/pact-for-the-future/

32 Smajic (2025) "Climate Change and Deep Seabed Mining: Implications of the COSIS Advisory Opinion", *Ocean Development & International Law*, 56(3), 415–450, https://doi.org/10.1080/00908320.2025.2536544

33 Burns (2025) *Mutually Reinforcing: How A Fossil Fuel Non-Proliferation Treaty Complements The Paris Agreement And UNFCCC*, https://fossilfueltreaty.org/research

34 UNFCCC "United Nations Framework on Convention on Climate Change, Article 4

Commitments", https://unfccc.int/files/cooperation_and_support/ldc/application/pdf/article4.pdf
35 Pacific Islands Development Forum (2015) "Suva Declaration on Climate Change" https://www.pidf.int/wp-content/uploads/2017/07/Suva-declaration-on-climate-change.pdf
36 LDC Climate Change (2017) *LDC Group Statement at the Joint closing session for COP23/CMP13/CMA1.2*, https://www.ldc-climate.org/ldc_chair_statement/ldc-group-statement-at-closing-of-cop23/
37 *The Lofoten Declaration: Climate Leadership Requires a Managed Decline of Fossil Fuel Production* (2017), https://lofotendeclaration.org
38 International Campaign to Abolish Nuclear Weapons (2025) http://www.icanw.org
39 Newell and Simms (2019) "Towards a fossil fuel non-proliferation treaty", *Climate Policy*, pp 1043–1054, https://www.tandfonline.com/doi/full/10.1080/14693062.2019.1636759
40 International Energy Agency (2024) "World Energy Investment 2024", https://www.iea.org/reports/world-energy-investment-2024/overview-and-key-findings
41 Vanuatu ICJ Initiative (2023) "Port Vila Call for a Just Transition to a Fossil Fuel Free Pacific", https://www.vanuatuicj.com/call
42 Naiuli Declaration (2022), https://ourcommonprayer.org/wp-content/uploads/2022/03/efe44-thenaiulideclarationforafossilfuelnon-proliferationtreaty.pdf
43 Women's International League for Peace and Freedom (2024) *Stop Fossil Fuels from Fuelling*

Conflict: Why the Fossil Fuel Non-Proliferation Treaty is an Essential Climate Tool for Peace, https://www.wilpf.org/publications/stop-fossil-fuels-from-fuelling-conflict-why-the-fossil-fuel-non-proliferation-treaty-is-an-essential-climate-tool-for-peace/

44 UN Environment Program (2023) *Production Gap Report 2023*, https://www.unep.org/resources/production-gap-report-2023

45 Fraser (2021) "Climates of capital for a trans-environmental eco-socialism", *New Left Review*, (127), 94–127

46 Trott et al. (2023) "People's action for climate justice: A systematic review", *Local Environment*, 28(9), 1131–1152

47 Sangaralingam (2024) "Time to End 'Waste Colonialism' Through a Global Plastics Treaty", *The Diplomat*, https://thediplomat.com/2024/03/time-to- end-waste-colonialism-through-a-global-plastics-treaty/; Madhanagopal et al. (2022) "Environment, Climate, and Social Justice: Interdisciplinary Voices from the Global South", *Environment, Climate, and Social Justice: Perspectives and Practices from the Global South*, pp 1–13

48 Crouzé et al. (2023) "Learning democracy through activism: the global climate strike movement and Belgian youth's democratic experience in times of environmental emergency", *Social Movement Studies*, 23(1), pp 56–71

49 Shim (2024) "Personalising climate change — how activists from Fridays for Future visualise climate action on Instagram", *Humanities and Social Sciences Communications*, 11(1), pp 1–9

50 Bohonos et al. (2019) "Using artistic expression as a

teaching strategy for social justice: Examining music from the Civil Rights and Black Lives Matter movements", *Advances in Developing Human Resources*, 21(2), pp 250–266

51 Fortes et al. (2023) "Contesting Extractivism through Amazonian Indigenous Artivism: Decolonial Reflections on Possibilities for Crafting a Pluriverse from within", *Alternautas*, 10(1), 155–190

52 Bohonos et al. (2019)

53 Francis (2015) "Encyclical Letter Laudato Si'"https://www.vatican.va/content/francesco/en/encyclicals/documents/papa-francesco_20150524_enciclica-laudato-si.html

54 Pacific Artists for Climate Justice (2025) "This is Our Home", https://www.fossilfreepacific.org

About The Australia Institute

The Australia Institute conducts research that drives the public debate and secures policy outcomes to make Australia better.

The Australia Institute's independence and nonpartisanship ensure our work is guided by a vision for a fairer Australia, without political or commercial influence. Our research regularly calls into question powerful vested interests, multinational corporations, and the economic orthodoxy.

This work is only possible because of independent donations. The support of our donors powers the Institute's ability to fulfil its motto: research that matters. To contribute to our work and ongoing research, you can make a donation on our website by scanning the QR code below.

Acknowledgements

This essay emerges from a long river of struggle, learning, listening, and unlearning. Like water itself, it has many sources — some visible, many unseen, some named here, many carried quietly in memory, experience, and conscience. What follows is therefore not only an acknowledgement of individuals, but a recognition of collective labour, shared courage, and intergenerational wisdom.

I wish first to acknowledge the countless people — known and unknown to me—whose ideas, actions, and sacrifices have shaped the thinking that flows through these pages. From frontline communities resisting extractivism, pollution, and dispossession; to Indigenous peoples defending water as sacred rather than a commodity; to workers, farmers, fisherfolk, and caregivers whose lives are disrupted first and worst by climate chaos — this essay is indebted to your lived realities. You have taught me, again and again, that climate justice is not an abstract debate about science and degrees, but a daily struggle for dignity, survival, and hope.

I am deeply grateful to the many activists, scholars, artists, journalists, faith leaders, movement builders, and trade unionists whose articles I have read, speeches I have listened to, conversations I have been privileged to be part of, and documentaries, poems, songs, and other creative expressions that have stirred both my heart and my political imagination. Arts and culture have always been essential to movements for justice, and this work carries the imprint of that creative courage — the ability to make us feel what statistics alone never can.

This essay is also shaped by the struggles I have been honoured to participate in alongside comrades across continents — those who stood with me in campaigns for human rights, environmental justice, and democratic accountability; those who challenged me when I was wrong; and those who modelled leadership rooted not in ego, but in service. I have learned as much from setbacks and failures as from victories, and I remain profoundly thankful to those who stayed in the struggle even when hope felt fragile.

In particular, I acknowledge the generations of climate justice advocates — especially from the Global South and Small Island States — who have insisted that the climate crisis is inseparable from histories of colonialism, racism, and economic exploitation. Their moral clarity has strengthened the call that runs through this essay: that protecting water, safeguarding life, and securing a just future for our children requires us to confront the root causes of the crisis. Central among these is the continued expansion of coal, oil, and gas. There is no credible pathway to climate justice, water security, or intergenerational fairness without a rapid, fair, and funded phase-out of fossil fuels.

This work has also been enriched by collaboration, care, and solidarity in very practical ways. I wish to thank Gabrielle Cabodil, a close collaborator on this essay, whose leadership, care, and intellectual contributions were invaluable throughout this journey. Her commitment reflects the courage and creativity of a new generation of movement leaders. *Mabuhay ang kabataan, manggagawa, at kababaihang Pilipino!*

My sincere thanks go to Pauline Fabrero and Anna Bonderenko, whose steadfast care, friendship, and quiet competence helped hold both the team and this work together with humanity and grace. Their labour — often unseen, always essential — made this project possible.

I am also deeply grateful to Becca Galvez, whose clarity of thought and depth of heart helped shape the direction of this essay from its earliest moments, and to Jesh Latchman, Nathalia Clark, and Michael Poland for their guidance, solidarity, and generous support along the way.

Finally, I wish to acknowledge my family and loved ones, who remind me — often without words — why this struggle matters. To all my family and friends: thank you for the love, patience, laughter, and grounding that sustain me. In moments of exhaustion or despair, you return me to what is most essential—that this fight for water, climate justice, and a liveable future is, at its core, an act of love. Love for people we know, and for those we may never meet; love for generations yet unborn; and love for this shared home that sustains us all.

As an African proverb reminds us: "If you want to go fast, go alone. If you want to go far, go together." This essay is offered in that spirit — aware of its limits, grounded in gratitude, and committed to the collective journey ahead.

The Australia Institute
Research that matters.
Celebrating 30 yrs of big ideas
AFTER AMERICA
WITH DR EMMA SHORTIS

FOLLOW
THE
MONEY

DOLLARS & SENSE
with Greg Jericho
The Australia Institute
Research that matters

What's the Big Idea?
with Paul Barclay

Vantage Point Issue 4

Read it and pass it on. Put your name and email below and start a conversation with other readers.

Name	Contact